Alix & Ted,

hopefully, you enjoy your Christmas
market tour in Germany and also
these impressions of Düsseldorf, my
home town for the past five years.
Of course, you are invited heartily!

Love, Svenja

Rothenburg ob der Tauber, December 3rd 2016

DÜSSELDORF HIGHLIGHTS

Fotos von Michael Rennertz · photos by Michael Rennertz

DROSTE

DAS BESTE VON DÜSSELDORF

Nordrhein-Westfalens Landeshauptstadt ist bei Einheimischen, Zugezogenen und Besuchern gleichermaßen beliebt: Die Düsseldorfer mögen ihr modernes und lebendiges Flair, die Touristen sind von ihrer Vielfalt und den Sehenswürdigkeiten, die fast alle fußläufig zu erreichen sind, beeindruckt. Nicht ohne Grund kommen jährlich über zwei Millionen Gäste in die elegante Rheinmetropole. Denn wo liegen modischer Schick, experimentelle Kunst und rheinische Lebensart schon so nah beieinander? In welcher Stadt sitzen internationales Publikum, betriebsame Geschäftsleute und alteingesessene Bürger zusammen und sind sich einig, dass es hier einfach am schönsten ist? Düsseldorf wartet deutschlandweit mit der höchsten Lebensqualität auf, weltweit rangiert die Landeshauptstadt sogar auf Platz 6 der Top-Wohlfühlmetropolen. Mit fast fünfzig Fachmessen genießt sie den Ruf einer Messestadt von Weltrang, mehr als hunderttausend Unternehmen haben sich in der Wirtschaftsregion Rhein-Ruhr angesiedelt.

Was liegt da näher, als die besten Sehenswürdigkeiten in einem Buch zu versammeln? Wir haben unsere persönlichen Highlights von Fotograf Michael Rennertz ins rechte Licht rücken lassen. Ob stylische Hafen-Szene oder gemütliche Altstadt-Atmosphäre, ehrwürdige Kirche oder moderne Kunst, mondänes Flanieren auf der Kö oder pure Lebensfreude bei einer der vielen schillernden Veranstaltungen – dieser Bildband zeigt die schönsten Seiten der Stadt.
Mit den Bildunterschriften auf Deutsch und Englisch wird er nicht nur für Gäste Düsseldorfs zum wertigen Andenken, sondern lässt auch jedem die Heimatstadt liebenden Düsseldorfer das Herz aufgehen.

Viel Freude beim Entdecken und Wiedersehen wünscht

Ihr Droste-Team

THE BEST OF DÜSSELDORF

Düsseldorf, capital city of the federal state of North Rhine-Westphalia, is equally popular among its inhabitants, newcomers and visitors to the city. People in Düsseldorf appreciate its modern and lively flair, tourists are impressed by the wide variety of places to go and sights to see that are almost all within walking distance. There is a reason why more than two million visitors come to this elegant city on the Rhine every year. Where else would you find fashionable chic, experimental art and the Rhenish lifestyle so close to each other? Which other city has an international clientele, bustling business people and natives of Düsseldorf all sitting together and agreeing that this is just the best place to be? Düsseldorf not only offers the best quality of life anyway in Germany, but also the state capital ranks sixth among the world's most liveable cities.
With almost fifty trade fairs, it has gained an international reputation, and more than a hundred thousand companies have set up their business in the economic region of Rhine and Ruhr.

What could be more obvious than compiling a book of the best sights?
We arranged for our personal highlights to be portrayed by photographer, Michael Rennertz. Whether a stylish port scene or comfy Old Town atmosphere, dignified churches or modern art, strolling along the fashionable Kö or the sheer joy of life at one of the many glamorous events – these photographs showcase the most beautiful parts of the city. With captions in German and English, it will serve as a delightful keepsake both for visitors of Düsseldorf and those inhabitants tied to their roots.

We hope you enjoy exploring and revisiting the highlights.

Your Droste Team

Rheinuferpromenade · Zwischen Burgplatz und Landtag erstreckt sich seit 1995 die Rheinuferpromenade mit ihrer Unteren und Oberen Werft. Nachdem eine vierspurige Bundesstraße unterirdisch zum Rheinufertunnel umgebaut wurde, gestalteten Architekten um Niklas Fritschi die nun frei gewordene Oberfläche zu einer preisgekrönten Flaniermeile. Auf der Unteren Werft bietet die Gastronomie in den »Kasematten« Speis und Trank – im Winter unter Heizpilzen. Der Blick auf die vorbeifahrenden Schiffe ist – zumindest was die anliegenden Residenzen betrifft – buchstäblich unbezahlbar. Nostalgisch mutet die Rheinpegel-Uhr an der Treppe zu den Kasematten an – innen befindet sich jedoch hochmoderne Technik, die den zum Rhein gewandten Betrachter über die aktuelle Wassertiefe des Flusses informiert.

Rheinuferpromenade · This fine and spacious walkway stretches from Burgplatz near the Old town down to the State Parliament. In 1995, the former four-lane road which had been crowded with traffic since the 60s was rebuilt as a tunnel and left room for Niklas Fritschi and his architect colleagues to design an award-winning promenade on its surface. The lower wharf features a number of outdoor restaurants which attract passers-by to have a meal or a drink. Whether you are a resident of one of the houses lining the promenade or just enjoy your drink below – the view onto the floating ships and the river is priceless. Don't let the nostalgic appearance of the clock fool you: the inner clockwork is a high-tech device which keeps the spectator up-to-date about the current water level.

Rheinuferpromenade · Bei gutem Wetter bevölkern zahlreiche Spaziergänger, Radfahrer und Petanque-Spieler die etwa 1 km lange Asphaltstrecke der Rheinufer- promenade. Die Promenade ist ebenfalls Schauplatz für abwechslungsreiche Veranstaltungen: Bücherpromenade, Japan-Tag und Metro-Group-Marathon sind einige der Highlights. Die rund 600 Platanen entlang der Promenade ziehen immer wieder interessierte Blicke auf sich, machen sie doch im Winter nach Verlust all ihrer Blätter einen geradezu nackten Eindruck.
Ein weiteres Phänomen kann man regelmäßig an Sommerabenden beobachten, wenn Scharen von hellgrünen Vögeln die Bäume bevölkern und laut kreischen. Es handelt sich dabei um Halsbandsittiche, die in den 60er-Jahren aus Indien einge- führt wurden und nicht nur die deutschen Winter überlebten, sondern sich seitdem in verschiedenen Städten am Rhein ausgebreitet haben.

Rheinuferpromenade · Sunny weekends attract loads of people taking walks, biking or playing petanque on the paved walkway stretching about 1 km along the bank of the Rhine river. In addition, the promenade stages a variety of events – a book fair, Japan Day, and MetroGroup marathon just to name a few. About 600 strange- looking trees alongside this promenade often provoke thought when losing all their leaves in wintertime and making an almost naked impression.
There is a further phenomenon regularly to be observed in summer nights – crowds of light-green birds are occupying those trees, screeching loudly. They are a type of ring-necked parakeet which were brought over from India during the 1960s. Not only did they survive German winters, they have also been spreading among several cities along the Rhine river.

Alter Hafen · Der »Alte Hafen« ist nicht zu verwechseln mit dem Düsseldorfer Medienhafen. Er liegt an der Stelle eines ehemaligen Hafenbeckens, in dem Rheinschiffe etwa im Winter Schutz vor Beschädigungen durch das Eis des Flusses fanden – dem sogenannten »Sicherheitshafen«. Wer genau hinsieht, stellt fest, dass es keine Verbindung mehr zum Rhein gibt. Auch der seit 1996 dort lagernde Aalschocker ist allenfalls eine filmreife Dekoration ohne historischen Ursprung.

Alter Hafen · Don't mix up the so-called Alte Hafen with Düsseldorf's modern Media Harbour. Previously it was used as a safety harbour by ships seeking retreat from ice in the Rhine river. Look closely to notice that the basin does not have a water connection to the Rhine river anymore. Call it fake or nostalgic – the fishing boat in this basin is also only an artificial reminiscence of old times.

12_13 ▽

Rheinwiese Oberkassel · In Düsseldorf liegen moderne Architektur, internationales Business und grüne Natur in direkter Nähe zueinander. Von der linken Rheinseite aus, die verächtlich auch die »schäl Sitt« genannt wird, kann man das Panorama der Rheinuferpromenade mit den Wahrzeichen der Stadt, Oberkasseler Brücke, Tonhalle, Lambertuskirche und Schlossturm, betrachten, während man die Ruhe der Oberkasseler Rheinwiesen genießt.

Oberkassel riverbank · In Düsseldorf, modern architecture, international business and beautiful green landscapes lie directly in the vicinity of each other. Even though the left side of the Rhine river is ironically called the wrong side, the view from here onto the skyline of the city centre including Oberkassel bridge, Tonhalle, St. Lambert church and the castle tower is the best you can get. It is easy to find peace and quiet while standing on the green meadowlands lining the riverbank.

Rheinkirmes · Auf den Oberkasseler Rheinwiesen findet seit 1901 jährlich in der dritten Juliwoche zehn Tage lang eine der größten Düsseldorfer Attraktionen statt. Die »Größte Kirmes am Rhein« zieht mit zahlreichen Fahrgeschäften und Bierzelten rund vier Millionen Besucher aus der Stadt, aber auch aus dem weiteren Umland an. Ausrichter des Festes ist der St.-Sebastianus-Schützenverein Düsseldorf 1316 e.V., der damit einerseits des Stadtpatrons Düsseldorfs, St. Apollinaris von Ravenna, und andererseits der Kirchweihe der St.-Lambertus-Basilika gedenkt.
Das Festprogramm folgt einem traditionellen Verlauf, der nicht nur durch einen historischen Schützenumzug, das Königsschießen und Festgottesdienste geprägt ist, sondern als Highlight am Freitagabend auch ein spektakuläres Feuerwerk bietet.

Rheinkirmes · The left riverside of the Rhine goes crazy every year in July.
Since 1901, the Rheinkirmes has been one of the biggest attractions of the city.
It is considered to be the largest fun-fair along the Rhine river. Its many rides and beer tents annually attract around four million visitors from in and around the city. The traditional shooting club St. Sebastianus Düsseldorf 1316 hosts the event in order to commemorate both Düsseldorf's patron saint St. Apollinaris of Ravenna and the church anniversary of St. Lambert, the first church of historic Düsseldorf. The agenda of the fun fair includes a historic parade, a shooting contest and celebratory church services. However, the absolute highlights is staged Friday night where thousands of spectators crowd the Rhine shore to watch the big fireworks.

Japan-Tag · An einem Samstag im Mai feiert Düsseldorf seit 2002 seine japanischen Einwohner. Die Stadt weist mit rund 8100 Personen die zweitgrößte japanische Gemeinde Europas auf. Düsseldorf bietet aufgrund seiner guten internationalen Verbindung und der günstigen Infrastruktur für viele Japaner einen attraktiven Wirtschaftsstandort – rund 450 japanische Unternehmen sind im größeren Umkreis der Stadt ansässig. Zahlreiche japanische Restaurants prägen ein Gebiet in der Innenstadt, während auf der anderen Rheinseite der Eko-Tempel und die japanische Schule ein japanisches Wohngebiet ausmachen.
Am Japan-Tag bieten auf der Rheinuferpromenade sowohl Akrobaten als auch Musiker und Köche einen faszinierenden Einblick in die japanische Kultur. Das Highlight gegen 23 Uhr ist ein Feuerwerk, bei dem sich japanische Pyrotechniker jeweils zu einem bestimmten Motto selbst übertreffen.

Japan Day · Düsseldorf has been celebrating Japan Day since 2002 as a special highlight every year in May. There are around 8,100 Japanese citizens living in Düsseldorf and the surrounding area and has thus the second-largest Japanese community in Europe. Around 450 Japanese companies have their German facilities in and around the city.
Japan Day has become a veritable highlight of the Düsseldorf event calendar. At the biggest German-Japanese festival of its kind, local Japanese people are intensively involved in shaping the festival. Acrobats, musicians and chefs offer a fascinating insight into their culture. The Japanese fireworks at night represents the outstanding highlight of the festival where Japanese pyrotechnicians reveal their extraordinary skills.

Schafe auf den Rheinwiesen · Auf der Oberkasseler Seite des Rheins kann man regelmäßig eine große Schafherde beobachten. Der Schäfer setzt eine Tradition seiner Familie fort, hat er sich doch in der dritten Generation dieser Aufgabe angenommen. Rund 1000 Tiere grasen das ganze Jahr über auf den Oberkasseler Rheinwiesen Richtung Heerdt – es sei denn, es ist im Winter so kalt, dass der Schäfer sie in einer zweieinhalbstündigen Wanderung über die Theodor-Heuss-Brücke Richtung Knittkuhl führt, wo er noch eine zweite Schafherde hat. Geschützt werden die Tiere nicht mehr mit einem Schäferhund, sondern durch einen Zaun, der einerseits spazieren geführte Hunde abhalten soll, andererseits auch die Schafe vor ungewollten Ausflügen bewahrt. Dass sie diese Grenze nicht immer respektieren, wird regelmäßig in der Zeitung dokumentiert.

Sheep on the riverbank · You might be surprised to find a flock of sheep grazing on the Oberkassel riverside so close to the centre of a city. In fact, its shepherd has been keeping up a tradition run by his family for three generations. The flock consists of about 1,000 animals which can be spotted throughout the whole year, unless harsh weather conditions force the shephard to take his flock on a walk of two and a half hours. He has them cross Theoder-Heuss Bridge and leads them to his home in Düsseldorf Knittkuhl where he owns a second flock of sheep. These days the animals are not protected by a dog any more, but by a fence intended to keep dogs out and sheep in. The media regularly report escapes from animals not having respected this rather fragile barrier.

Landtag und Yachthafen · Seit 1946 ist Düsseldorf Landeshauptstadt. Die englische
Besatzung hatte die Stadt aufgrund ihrer wirtschaftsgeografischen und verkehrsgüns-
tigen Lage und der im Gegensatz zum größeren Nachbarn Köln noch vorhandenen
Verwaltungsgebäude dazu bestimmt. Der Landtag war zuvor im ehemaligen Ständehaus und heutigen Museum K21 untergebracht.
Direkt nebenan liegt eingebettet in das nun zur Innenstadt abgeschlossene Hafenbecken ein kleiner Yachthafen.

State Parliament and marina · Düsseldorf has been the state capitol of North Rhine-
Westphalia since 1946. The British occupying forces had chosen Düsseldorf to take
over this role – not only for geographical reasons, but also because Düsseldor's
infrastructure and administrative buildings had not been destroyed as much as those
in nearby Cologne. The state parliament was previously located in what is today the
K21 Museum.
Between the state parliament and the basin constituting the Media Harbour, there is
an idyllic little marina.

22_23 ▽

Gehry-Bauten · Die offizielle Adresse dieser drei spektakulären Gebäude lautet
»Zollhof 1-3«, da sich an dieser Stelle im Medienhafen der Zollbereich des ehe-
maligen Industriehafens befand. Frank O. Gehry, einer der bekanntesten Architekten
der Welt, entwickelte 1994 eine Bauwerk-Trilogie von internationaler Bedeutung.
Die drei asymmetrischen Gebäude erhalten durch die Verwendung unterschiedlicher
Materialien und Formen jeweils eine eigene Identität.

Gehry Buildings · The postal address of these spectacular three buildings is Zollhof
1-3, which refers to the original customs area that was located on this piece of
property of the former industrial harbour. In 1994, one of the world's most famous
architects, Frank O. Gehry, designed a trilogy of buildings which achieved international recognition. He developed three different shapes each consisting of
different materials, giving them their individual appearances.

Neues Stadttor · Mit dem Bau des Rheinufertunnels 1993 hatte man Düsseldorfs Innenstadt auf einen Schlag bis zum Hafengebiet erweitert. Er endet genau unter dem »Neuen Stadttor«, das in Anlehnung an frühere Stadttore in der Altstadt den Eingang zum neuen Innenstadtbereich kennzeichnen soll. Das 75 m hohe Bürogebäude hat eine trapezförmigen Grundfläche und einen Hohlkörper in der Mitte. Es besteht von innen aus Stahl, Holz und Stein und ist durch eine doppelschalige Glasfassade ummantelt, die ein energiesparendes Klimasystem darstellt. 1996 gewann das Neue Stadttor bei den MIPIM Awards sowohl den Preis für das beste Bürogebäude als auch für das beste Gebäude überhaupt. Teile der Landesregierung sind in den oberen Stockwerken des Gebäudes untergebracht, das sich in unmittelbarer Nähe zum NRW-Landtag befindet.

New City Gate · In 1993, Düsseldorf's city centre underwent a significant expansion through the relocation of the four-lane road that had formerly been running along the Rhine river into a tunnel. This tunnel ends directly beneath the New City Gate near the Media Harbour, signifying the building as the new entrance to its main places of interest. The office building measures 75 m in total, has a trapeze-shaped base and a hollow body in the centre. While its core is made from steel, wood and stone, it is shelled by a double-layered glass facade which funktions as energy-saving air conditioning. The impressive building won the MIPIM Award for best office building and best building overall. Its vicinity to the state parliament makes it convenient for part of the state government to rent office space on some of the City Gates top floors.

Hyatt Regency-Hotel · Eine prominente Lage an der Hafenspitze des Medienhafens hat seit Ende 2010 ein 5-Sterne-Hotel inne. Das Hyatt Regency besticht vor allem durch Aussicht und Design. Die Gäste genießen sowohl einen Blick auf die moderne Architektur des Medienhafenbeckens als auch auf die bekannte Silhouette der Altstadt. Der untere Teil des Hotels erinnert an ein Schiff. Seitlich vom Hotel befindet sich die raumschiffartig anmutende Champagnerbar „Pebbles".

Hyatt Regency Hotel · The peninsula that makes up one side of the Media Harbour's main basin is occupied by a five-star hotel. The Hyatt Regency offers its guests lots of features to indulge in – the stunning view both on the Media Harbour's fascinating architecture and the silhouette of the Old town. The modern interior design is displayed in the luxury spa-area or the top-floor breakfast room. Large focus is also laid on the restaurant DOX and as well as a separate champagne-bar Pebbles.

28_29 ▽

Medienhafen · Die »bunte« Seite des Hafenbeckens bietet eine gelungene Mischung aus neuen und alten Gebäuden – die Stadt legte beim Umbau des ehemaligen Industriehafens Wert auf die Erinnerung an seine ursprüngliche Funktion. Hervorstechende Elemente in der Fassade sind u.a. die »Flossies« – Plastikfiguren in knalligen Farben, die überlebensgroß das Gebäude hochklettern. Die Künstlerin Rosalie hatte die Flossies 1998 anlässlich der Eröffnung des Kunststoffmuseums im Ehrenhof erschaffen.

Media Harbour · Displaying a colourful mix of old-style and modern buildings, the city wants to commemorate the formerly industrial use of today's Media Harbour. The Flossies are one of the most striking features of the facade. The oversized plastics are found to climb up the wall of a building. They were created by artist Rosalie on the occasion of the opening of Düsseldorf's new plastic museum in 1998.

Rheinturm · Der 1982 eröffnete ehemalige Fernmeldeturm ist mit das bekannteste Wahrzeichen Düsseldorfs und steht genau zwischen Medienhafen und Altstadt. Bis zur Spitze misst der Turm 240,5 m. Besucher, die »auf 180« sind, befinden sich auf etwa dieser Höhe im gleichnamigen Dreh-Restaurant (nachmittags und abends) mit je nach Wetterlage besserer oder schlechterer Aussicht. Wer »nur gucken« will, fährt mit dem Aufzug bis zur Aussichtsplattform knapp unterhalb des Restaurants. Besonderheit des Turms ist die von außen gut sichtbare, größte Dezimaluhr der Welt: An 39 von 62 beleuchteten Bullaugen können »eingeweihte« Beobachter die Uhrzeit ablesen. Zu bestimmten Zeiten leuchten die LEDs in den Farben der olympischen Ringe – ein Überbleibsel aus der Zeit, als sich Düsseldorf als Ausrichter für die Olympischen Spiele 2012 beworben hat.

Rhine Tower · One of the most popular tourist attractions was originally built to be a broadcasting tower. Positioned directly between the Media Harbour and the Old Town, it measures 240,5 m from bottom to top and has become a major landmark in Düsseldorf's skyline. Nowadays, visitors are invited to take the lift up to either the sightseeing platform or to the revolving restaurant. If you are daring enough, you may lie on the slanted glass windows and enjoy a view over the region. Look from almost anywhere in the city centre to see another important feature of the tower visible from the outside. Visible in the dark, world's largest decimal clock made up of 39 illuminated portholes runs up the tower. Try to figure out the time just by counting the lights! If you are lucky, you might even catch them changing colours, a reminder of Düsseldorf's bid to host the 2012 Olympic Games.

Apollo-Varieté-Theater · Seit 1997 erfreut das »Roncalli's Apollo-Varieté-Theater« am Rheinufer seine Besucher mit einem abwechslungsreichen Programm aus Akrobatik, Komödie und Magie. Leitender Architekt des ins Auge stechenden Baus genau unter- halb der Rhein-Knie-Brücke war Niklaus Fritschi, der kurz zuvor schon die Rheinufer- promenade geplant hatte und für die Realisierung des Gesamtkonzepts den Deutschen Städtebaupreis erhielt. Die bewegliche Bühnenrückwand lässt sich zur Freude der Zuschauer während der Vorstellungen zur effektvollen Aussicht auf den Rhein öffnen. Gründer und Betreiber ist Zirkusdirektor Bernhard Paul, der nach seiner Karriere als Art Director den Zirkus Roncalli mitbegründete und von Zeit zu Zeit als Clown »Zippo« selbst auf der Bühne stand.

Apollo Varietié Theater · If you feel like watching a thrilling combination of acrobats, magicians and comedians, Roncallis Apollo Varietié Theater just underneath Rhein- Knie-Bridge is the place to go. Since 1997 the founder, ringmaster and clown Bernhard Paul and his cast have been fascinating their audience with regularly changing performances. As a special feature, the stage wall is sometimes opened to reveal a stunning view on the Rhine river. Niklaus Fritschi, the architect responsible for designing the building had received a national urban development award for planning the city's Rhine embankment promenade.

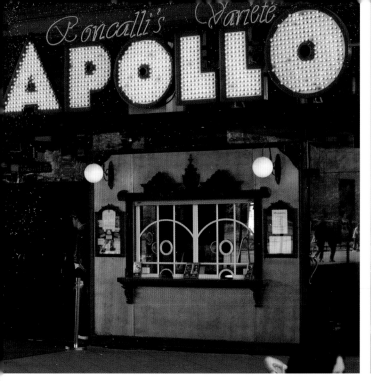

Hafenblick · Zwischen Rheinuferpromenade und Medienhafen zweigt rechts ein Spazierweg Richtung Industriehafen ab, der über eine Brücke zum Golf-Sport-Verein auf der Lausward und Düsseldorfs kleinem Badestrand führt. Von der Brücke aus hat man eine gute Aussicht auf den stromabwärts fließenden Rhein. Hier kann man sowohl Frachtschiffe zwischen Duisburg und Köln als auch Ausflugsschiff beobachten, die Touristen auf einer kurzweiligen Panorama-Tour an den Sehenswürdigkeiten des Rheinufers und des Medienhafens vorbeiführen. Im rechten, seit der Umgestaltung des Hafens geschlossenen Hafenbecken liegt ein kleiner Yachthafen.
Hier befindet sich alljährlich im Juli der Start zum Düsseldorfer Triathlon, bei dem Teilnehmer die erste Disziplin im Hafenbecken absolvieren.

View from the harbour bridge · If you want to hit the beach in Düsseldorf, head from Rhine embankment promenade towards the Media Harbour and keep right to cross a bridge leading past Düsseldorf's industrial harbour area towards a golf club. Don't expect too much in terms of swimming and sunbathing, but instead stay on the bridge for a while to catch a view on the Rhine flowing downstream. Watch cargoships traveling between Duisburg and Cologne as well as cruise ships taking tourists on a sightseeing tour along the highlights of the harbour area. On your right-hand side you will see the basin that was closed off towards the Rhine river in order to construct the modern Media Harbour. Participants of Düsseldorf's annually staged triathlon complete their first event in this basin.

Schlossturm · Der Schlossturm direkt am Rheinufer hat in der »Skyline« der Düsseldorfer Altstadt einen festen Platz. Fest steht er als einziges Überbleibsel des sich
einst auf dem Burgplatz befindenden Schlosses. Die ursprüngliche gräfliche Burg
von 1260 spiegelte während der nächsten Jahrhunderte die Geschichte des Dorfes
an der Düssel wider, war sie doch zwischenzeitlich Residenzschloss der Kurfürsten
um Jan Wellem und seiner Vorfahren. Nach seinem vierten Brand 1872 entschied
man sich zum endgültigen Abriss. Heute sind im Schlossturm ein Schifffahrtsmuseum
sowie ein Café mit idyllischem Ausblick untergebracht. Unterhalb der Freitreppe,
die im Sommer bei jungen Leuten beliebter Aufenthaltsort ist, mündet der nördliche
Arm des kleinen Flusses, der Düsseldorf seinen Namen gab, in den Rhein –
die Düssel.

Castle Tower · The Castle Tower is a prominent element of the city's skyline.
It is the only remainder of the former castle which used to be located on Burgplatz
directly by the Rhine river. Before it was torn down in 1872 after burning for the
fourth time, it closely witnessed the history of the small, but constantly expanding
village by the Düssel river. During its most glamorous time, it was residence to Prince
Elector Jan Wellem and his family. Nowadays, a visit inside is worthwhile: Take a
look at the Shipping Museum or indulge in coffee and cake right under the rooftop
in a neat café offering a beautiful view over the Old Town and the Rhine. If you
prefer spending time outside, why not do as the locals do and sit on the steps at the
foot of the tower where the Düssel flows into the Rhine.

Radschlägerbrunnen · Auf dem Burgplatz befindet sich umgeben von rustikaler Gastronomie ein Brunnen mit dem wohl bekanntesten Symbol Düsseldorfs – dem Radschläger. Zwei kleine Jungen (der Künstler verwendete 1954 übrigens zweimal dasselbe Gesicht) verkörpern das, was im 19. Jahrhundert unter geschäftstüchtigen Burschen üblich war: Sie schlugen ein Rad vor den die Stadt immer zahlreicher besuchenden Handelsreisenden und verdienten sich so »eene Pennig«. Düsseldorf erinnert auf Gullideckeln, durch Statuen und mit dem alljährlich am Rheinufer stattfindenden Radschlägerwettbewerb für Kinder an diesen Brauch. Laut einer Legende entstand die lustige Tollerei nach einer spontanen Hilfe-Aktion: Ein Junge leistete akrobatischen Ersatz für das zerbrochene Kutschrad des durch die Stadt fahrenden Kurfürsten Jan Wellem.

Cartwheelers · Located under a group of trees right next to a restaurant on one side of Burgplatz, there is a water fountain featuring Düsseldorf's most famous symbol. Two little boys (by the way, the artist gave the very same face to both statues) resemble an activity very common among young boys during the 19th century. They performed cartwheels in front of merchants visiting the city to do business here, hoping to earn a few pennies of this. You can find reminiscences of this all over Düsseldorf: printed on gully covers, as statues, as souvenir pins and live in the annual children's cartwheel contest. According to a legend, this acrobatic habit evolved from the spontaneous action of a boy when Prince Elector Jan Wellem's coach lost one of its wheels while he was riding through town. The boy jumped to help out as a wheel.

St. Lambertus · Im Stadtbild nicht fehlen darf der schiefe Turm der romanischen Basilika, die zur Stadtgründung 1288 ihren Status als Stiftskirche erhielt. Der Vorgängerbau einer Kapelle ist zu dieser Zeit schon urkundlich erwähnt. Seine verdrehte Form verdankt der Turmhelm der Tatsache, dass bei einem Wiederaufbau im Jahr 1815 das verwendete Holz noch zu feucht war und sich verzog. Auch eine Legende rankt sich um diese Eigenheit – der Teufel soll aus Wut beim Versuch, die Kirche herauszureißen, den Turm verdreht haben. Innen birgt die Kirche ebenfalls allerlei Schätze: Im 14. Jahrhundert wurde das Bestreben, Düsseldorf zum Wallfahrtsort zu machen, mit der Überführung der Reliquien des Hl. Apollinaris, Stadtpatron Düsseldorfs, aus Remagen unterstützt. Ferner liegen in ihr mehrere Mitglieder der herzoglichen Familie von Jülich-Kleve-Berg begraben.

St. Lambertus · This sight always makes passers-by wonder. Near Burgplatz and just next to the Schlossturm, the church tower of St. Lambert, a Roman basilica, rises up above most other rooftops. However, it is crooked. This is due to the fact that the tower was reconstructed after burning down in 1815, but the wooden material was still too moist which caused its twisted appearance. There is also a legend that when he found out about the construction of a new catholic church, the devil tried to pull out the church, twisting its top in the process. The church, which was the first one situated in Düsseldorf when it was declared a town, also holds some precious treasures inside. The bones of the city's patron St. Apollinaire are buried here as well as those of some members of the ducal family Jülich-Kleve-Berg.

Jan Wellem · Als wohl berühmtester Kurfürst der Stadt gilt Johann Wilhelm von Pfalz-Neuburg (1679-1716), im Volksmund »Jan Wellem« genannt. Seine politischen Fähigkeiten gelten als umstritten. Zahlreiche heute noch vorhandene Institutionen belegen jedoch, dass er trotz karger finanzieller Mittel der Stadt ein großer Förderer von Kunst und Kultur war. Gemeinsam mit seiner Frau Anna Maria Luisa de Medici baute er z.B. die erste Gemäldegalerie und das erste Opernhaus der Stadt auf. Nicht zuletzt durch seinen großen Hofstaat rund ums Schloss sorgte er für viele Arbeitsaufträge. Das Volk ehrte ihn mit der Errichtung des Reiterstandbildes, das sich zentral auf dem Marktplatz vor dem Rathaus in der Altstadt befindet. Das historische Rathaus, dessen ältester Teil aus dem 16. Jahrhundert stammt, bietet besonders im abendlich angestrahlten Zustand ein romantisches Bild.

Jan Wellem · Düsseldorf commemorates Johann Wilhelm von Pfalz-Neuburg (1679-1716) as their most famous Prince Elector. Though not being the strongest political statesman, he did become famous for some other great achievements he made in his lifetime. Strongly interested in culture and arts, he was the initiator of many institutions still visible in the city today in some way or the other. With the support of his second wife Anna Maria Luisa de Medici, he can be held responsible for building the first art gallery and the first opera house. His huge court brought about many jobs in and around the castle. As a lover of glamour and luxury, he had the people erect a bronze statue of himself right in front of the historic town hall. The nostalgic-looking street lights surrounding the statue are another reminiscence of his luminous age.

Karneval · Dass in Düsseldorf gerne gefeiert wird, beweist alljährlich die Karnevals-
saison. Pünktlich am 11.11. um 11:11 Uhr wird sie offiziell vom hiesigen Clown des
Karnevals, dem »Hoppeditz«, eingeläutet. Die heißesten Tage finden üblicherweise
im Februar von Gründonnerstag, auch als »Altweiber« bekannt, bis Aschermittwoch
statt. Feste Programmpunkte sind mittlerweile die Erstürmung des Rathauses durch
die Frauen an Altweiber, der »Tuntenlauf« am Karnevalssamstag und der Straßen-
karneval auf der Königsallee am Karnevalssonntag. Den Höhepunkt bildet seit
1834 der Rosenmontagszug, bei dem in den verkleideten Massen in der Innenstadt,
die den kunstvoll geschmückten Motto-Wagen zujubeln, kein Durchkommen ist.
Die Traditionen werden durch zahlreiche Karnevalsvereine und das Karnevals-
museum gepflegt.

Carneval · Düsseldorf is one good place to party – that's for sure. One of the times
when this becomes most evident is during the season of carnival. Each year on
11 November at 11 past 11, it is officially opened by "Hoppeditz", Düsseldorf's
clown of carnival. The season lasts for half a year, but the highlight of this period
takes place on five days in February. From Green Tuesday to Ash Wednesday,
the town goes crazy, indulging in colourful costumes, parades and heavy drinking.
A gay's event on Saturday and street carnival on Königsallee on Sunday have
become constant elements on the agenda. Since 1834, the highlight of these crazy
days has taken place on Rose Monday – a long parade of colourfully decorated
coaches is cheered on by the dressed-up crowds. The City Carnival Museum and
many carnival clubs cherish the traditions year in and year out.

Weihnachtsmarkt · Über die Grenzen der Stadt hinaus bekannt, erfreut der Düsseldorfer Weihnachtsmarkt auf verschiedenen Plätzen in der Altstadt ein bunt gemisch-
tes Publikum. Besonderheit sind hier die unterschiedlichen Ausgestaltungen der
jeweiligen Weihnachtsdörfchen – so gibt es u.a. den »Engelchenmarkt« am Carsch-
Haus, den »Sternchen-Markt« im Innenhof des Wilhelm-Marx-Hauses und den Markt
auf der Flinger Straße, dessen Buden den Bürgerhäusern nachempfunden sind.
Bekannt für guten Glühwein ist der Markt vor dem Rathaus, Kunsthandwerk findet
man vorwiegend auf der Schadowstraße. Insgesamt etwa 210 Buden bieten den
vielen Besuchern ein Vergnügen aus internationalen kulinarischen Weihnachts-
Spezialitäten und -schmuck. Organisierter Weihnachtsmarkttourismus sorgt auch
in den umliegenden Geschäften und Kneipen für ein gutes Geschäft.

Christmas Market · During Christmas time, Düsseldorf has become quite famous for
staging one of the nicest Christmas markets in Germany. The fact that the "market"
is made up of several Christmas villages spread all over the city centre makes
it especially attractive. Their names describe the different types of decoration that
they focus on – stars, angels and traditional village-style houses let every visitor find
their favourite. Don't leave the Christmas market without having tried a cup of mulled
wine, which is an alcoholic fruit punch which warms your heart. One of the stands in
front of the town hall is supposed to be selling the best one available. Of course
there is much more to purchase in one of the 210 stands. Potato pancakes with
apple sauce, handmade Christmas decoration, and flammkuchen will get you in
the mood for the holidays!

Altstadt · Gaslaternen und Kopfsteinpflaster sind in Düsseldorf hart umkämpfte Reliquien aus früherer Zeit. Die Gaslaternen, mit deren Errichtung sich übrigens Kurfürst Jan Wellem beliebt machte, sorgen für nostalgischen Charme in der Stadt. Aus ökonomischen Gründen möchte die Stadt sie durch LED-Leuchten ersetzen – ein Ansinnen, das eine riesige Petitions-Aktion unter den Bürgern hervorrief. Ein weiteres Element der Straßen, die seit der Stadterweiterung die Düsseldorfer Altstadt ausmachen, ist das Kopfsteinpflaster, das jedoch nach und nach durch Betonsteinplatten in Granitoptik ersetzt wird. Die Stadt nutzte umfangreiche Kanalsanierungen ebenfalls zur Neugestaltung der Wege und »Möblierung« der Innenstadtstraßen. Rund um die Maxkirche und das Traditionsrestaurant »Schiffchen« findet man noch Kopfste-n-pflaster und Gaslaternen.

Old Town · Street lamps fuelled by gas and cobblestone pavements are two reminiscences from the old times which have been an issue during the past years. Gas-fuelled lamps were first introduced by Prince Elector Jan Wellem who was very popular among his people. They create a nostalgic kind of atmosphere wherever you walk past them. For economic reasons, the government wants to replace them by LED lamps – an intention that has evoked numerous activities of protest among residents. The replacement of the cobblestone pavement in the city centre's pedestrian area is another major issue which arouses discontent. The city used the reconstruction of the sewers to kick off the replacement of the former cobblestones by concrete paving stone. Take a walk to the area around Maxkirche to spot some old-fashioned street lamps or cobblestone pavements in the Old Town.

Carlsplatz · Laut Straßenschild befindet sich der »Marktplatz« zwar vor dem Rathaus, aber schon seit vielen Jahren findet der »schönste Markt Nordrhein-Westfalens« etwa 500 m entfernt auf dem Carlsplatz statt. Hier entdeckt der Besucher nicht nur frische heimische Obst- und Gemüsesorten, sondern Exotik bis hin zu essbaren Blüten. Wen bei dem reichhaltigen Angebot der schnelle Hunger packt, hat die Qual der Wahl zwischen Fischspezialitäten, indischem Essen, französischen Backwaren, Düsseldorfer Hausmannskost in Form von Suppen und italienischen Speisen. So exotisch einige weit gereiste Früchte sind, auf Düsseldorfer Spezialitäten in Form von ABB-Senf wird ebenfalls nicht verzichtet. Unter dem Carlsplatz befand sich im Zweiten Weltkrieg übrigens ein Bunker, der später als Kino und mittlerweile als Lagerraum für die Markt-Anbieter genutzt wird.

Carlsplatz · The street sign reads market place, but in order to shop at North Rhine-Westphalia's most beautiful market, you need to keep walking for another 500 m to reach Carlsplatz. Fruit and vegetables from local farms please the customers' eye just as much as exotic fruits. Have you ever eaten flowers? Well, here you can. Don't worry if you get hungry in the presence of such abundance of food – there are also lots of stands offering a variety of delicious hot takeaway meals. Not only will you find different types of fish dishes, Indian curries, French pastries and local specialties are available as well. Decide for yourself if you prefer the exotic, much-traveled pineapples and dragon fruits, or if you go for Düsseldorfs locally produced mustard ("ABB-Senf") as a souvenir. Can you imagine that the basement below Carlsplatz used to be a bunker in WWII?

Uerige · Seit einem Lied der Kult-Band »Die Toten Hosen« gilt Düsseldorf als »längste Theke der Welt«. Es handelt sich dabei jedoch nicht etwa um eine einzige Theke, sondern spielt auf die Tatsache an, dass sich auf kleinstem Raum 260 Gastronomiebetriebe und Kneipen aneinanderreihen. Fester Bestandteil sind vier alteingesessene Hausbrauereien, die seit dem 19. Jahrhundert den Besucher mit dem hiesigen obergärigen Bier erfreuen. Eine davon ist das »Uerige«, benannt nach seinem einstigen griesgrämigen Wirt. Mit zum Inventar der rheinischen Hausbrauereien gehören die ruppigen Kellner, auch »Köbesse« genannt, die ungefragt dafür sorgen, dass der Gast stets ein volles Glas vor der Nase stehen hat. Sein Pendant ist der »Zappes«, der am Bierfass dem Köbes ausschenkt.

Uerige · Crowds of weekend tourists who come to Düsseldorf are aiming for the same destination – "the world's longest bar". The term was coined in a song by a very popular German band, the Tote Hosen. It actually does not refer to an single counter, but rather to the fact that Düsseldorf features around 260 bars, pubs, and restaurants lining the streets of the Old Town. A very important element here are four genuine home breweries which have been pleasing their guests with their own brand of Altbier, a local brew produced in a top-fermentation technique since the 19th century. The Uerige is one of those four home breweries and was named after its grumpy (urig) host centuries ago. Don't be irritated to find the waiters rather pushy and rude than attentive and friendly – it is part of a »Köbesse's« game to serve you without being asked.

Füchschen · Auf der Ratinger Straße geht es ein wenig gesitteter zu als wenige Hundert Meter weiter in der Bolkerstraße. Hier trifft sich das Düsseldorfer »Bildungs-bürgertum«, um gepflegt beim Altbier zusammenzusitzen. Eine der vier alteingeses-senen Hausbrauereien der Altstadt befindet sich hier – das »Füchschen«. Nicht nur in der Brauerei selbst, sondern auch in anderen Lokalen wie etwa der »Uel«, kann man es konsumieren. Beliebt ist die Stube auch bei internationalen Touristen, die sich hier an die rheinländisch-deftigen Spezialitäten auf der Speisekarte wagen und durch üppige Portionen erfreut werden.
Bekannt ist die Ratinger Straße auch noch aus einem anderen Grund: Die Toten Hosen begannen hier in den 70er-Jahren ihre einzigartige Karriere. Als traditioneller Ausgehtag für die Einheimischen hat sich auf »der Ratinger« der Mittwoch einge-bürgert.

Füchschen · If you are tired of the drunken party people crowding Bolkerstraße on weekend nights, proceed to Ratinger Straße to enjoy your beer in a more sophis-ticated surroundings. One of the four traditional home breweries is located on Ratinger Straße. Füchschen means little fox – a picture often used in their excellent marketing that you come across throughout town. The beer itself is also served in other bars and restaurants on and beyond Ratinger Straße. Mix both with locals and international guests enjoying hearty meals typical for the Rhineland area. It has become a habit for locals to meet for an after-work beer on Wednesday nights. Ratinger Straße has also gathered fame in the 1970s as the origin of German Punk – the most famous example being represented by the internationally renowned band Tote Hosen who had their first performances here.

Schumacher · Das »Schumacher Alt« gilt als das »älteste Altbier« Düsseldorfs.
Die obergärige Spezialität mit der malzigen Note wird seit 1838 hergestellt – seit
1902 geschieht dies im sogenannten Stammhaus auf der Oststraße. Der traditions-
reichste Brauereiausschank »Im Goldenen Kessel« befindet sich jedoch auf der
Bolkerstraße mitten in der Altstadt und bietet neben dem bernsteinfarbenen Getränk,
das übrigens laut Reinheitsgebot von 1516, dem ältesten deutschen Lebensmittelge-
setz, nur aus Malz, Hopfen und Wasser besteht, auch Deftiges aus der rheinischen
Küche. Das Unternehmen hält seine Familientradition in der Geschäftsführung schon
über Generationen hinweg aufrecht; Nina Thea Ungermann ist nach Thea Schnitzler
schon die zweite weibliche Geschäftsführerin.

Schumacher · The name Altbier was first introduced by the home brewery
Schumacher to describe the local alcoholic specialty being brewed using a top
fermentation technique. Schumacher have been producing it since 1838. Two major
locations belong to this brand – one is the first premises on Ostraße, including the
production site, the other one is the Goldener Kessel in the heart of the Old Town
on Bolkerstraße. Both serve beer as well as hearty dishes typical for the area.
The German Beer Purity Act dates back to 1516 and states that German beer is
allowed to contain only malt, water, hops and yeast – a law strictly followed by
all the home breweries. Family ties are very strong among the Schumachers –
the business has been in family hands since the start. Current CEO Nina Thea
Ungermann is not the first lady in this business to hold this position.

Zum Schlüssel · In bester Altstadtlage findet der durstige Düsseldorf(-besuch-)er die seit 1850 bestehende Hausbrauerei »Zum Schlüssel«. Das naturbelassene obergärige Bier mit dem milden, vollmundigen Geschmack wurde bereits zweimal beim »European Beer Star« mit der Goldmedaille ausgezeichnet. Der Name des Hauses ist auf eine frühere Tradition zurückzuführen: Am Ende der Bolkerstraße befand sich lange Zeit eines der Stadttore. Den Schlüssel dazu deponierte man allabendlich in einem nahe gelegenen Gasthaus, welches sich in der Bolkerstraße direkt neben dem heutigen »Zum Schlüssel« befand.
Im Sommer nutzt die Brauerei den gegenüberliegenden Kirchhof der Neanderkirche für seine Gäste. Sie ist eine von zwei evangelischen Altstadt-Kirchen, die im 17. Jahrhundert noch hinter den normalen Häuserreihen zurückstehen mussten.

Zum Schlüssel · Just across the street from Schumacher on Bolker Straße, another traditional home brewery attracts locals and tourists day in day out. The top-fermented Schlüssel-Altbier can be described as mild and full-bodied and has twice been awarded the Gold Medal at the European Beer Star contest. The key ("Schlüssel") which gave its name to the brewery dates back to a habit centuries old. Bolkerstraße used to be closed off by one of the city gates. These were locked at night and the keys would be deposited in the nearest pub. This was located in direct vicinity to today's Schlüssel brewery.
During the summer, guests can enjoy their Schlüssel beer and food in the churchyard right across the street. It belongs to Neanderkirche, which is one of two protestant churches in the Old Town dating back to the 17th century.

Schneider Wibbel · Der Mundartdichter Hans Müller-Schlösser erfreute 1913
das Düseldorfer Theaterpublikum mit einem Stück über »Schneider Wibbel«.
Die Geschichte des Schneidermeisters spielt zur Zeit der französischen Besatzung
der Stadt. Wegen Beleidigung des Kaisers Napoleon soll er eine Haftstrafe absitzen,
schickt jedoch an seiner Stelle seinen Gesellen, der während der Haft verstirbt.
Der Schneider beobachtet hinter einem Fenster seinen eigenen Leichenzug und kehrt
später als sein Zwillingsbruder in die Stadt zurück. Die auch durch ihre spanischen
und argentinischen Restaurants bekannte Schneider-Wibbel-Gasse im Herzen der
Altstadt erinnert u.a. mit einer Uhr an die Bühnenfigur. An einer Hauswand kann
man auch ein Relief der Leichenzugszene sehen.

Schneider Wibbel · A tailor named Wibbel is the main character of a play written
by Hans Müller-Schlösser, a local writer, in 1913. The story is set in early 19th-cen-
tury Düsseldorf, when the city was occupied by the French. The tailor is sentenced
to prison for having insulted their general, Napoleon Bonaparte. He sends his clerk
to serve the sentence for him. The clerk, however, dies while in jail. Standing behind
his window, Wibbel watches the funeral cortege walk by. This scene is displayed in
a relief picture on a house wall in Schneider-Wibbel-Gasse. Among the Spanish
and Argentinian restaurants which this little street is lined with, there is also a clock
with a little window underneath, revealing the tailor in his typical sitting posture.

Jazz Rally · Seit 1993 erlebt man in Düsseldorf drei Tage im Frühsommer Jazz vom Feinsten. Die Jazz Rally ist mit mittlerweile über 250.000 Besuchern das meistfrequentierte Jazz-Festival Deutschlands. Seine besondere Anziehungskraft macht u.a. die Tatsache aus, dass die etwa 100 Veranstaltungen fast alle fußläufig zueinander mit nur einem einzigen zu erwerbenden Eintrittsbutton zu erreichen sind. Regie führt seit den 90er-Jahren Klaus Doldinger, der nicht nur als Jazzmusiker, sondern auch als Komponist von Filmmusik bekannt ist – »Das Boot«, »Die unendliche Geschichte«, der »Tatort« und »Ein Fall für zwei« wurden durch seine Werke bereichert. Gemeinsam mit Udo Lindenberg gründete er die Band »Passport«, mit der er immer wieder bei der Jazz Rally auftritt.

Jazz Rally · Since 1993 Düsseldorf has been staging the most-frequented German jazz festival. The Jazz Rally attracts more than 250,000 visitors which raid the city centre for three days every year in May or June. The fact that buying just one admission chip grants access to about 100 events which are all located closely to each other makes the festival especially attractive. For many years the festival has been led by Klaus Doldinger, musician and composer, who gained fame by creating the music for movies such as "The Never-Ending Story" and "The Boat" and for several popular German TV serials. See him play in his band Passport which he founded together with Udo Lindenberg, another popular German singer.

Kunstverein · Rund um Grabbeplatz und Ehrenhof liegt Düsseldorfs »Museumsmeile«. In einem wuchtigen grauen Quaderbau gegenüber dem K20 hat der Kunstverein sein Zuhause. Gemeinsam von Bürgern und Künstlern 1829 gegründet, steht die junge und zeitgenössische Kunst, welche immer wieder durch bedeutende Ausstellungen unterstützt wird, im Mittelpunkt. Im selben Gebäude befindet sich die »Kunsthalle«.

Kunstverein · You could call it Museum Mile – the area between the Old Town, Rhine river and Hofgarten is clearly marked by the arts. Grabbeplatz and Ehrenhof are the two major hubs clustered with art institutions. A grey cube building at Grabbeplatz is home to an institution they founded in 1829 – the Kunstverein. Its changing exhibitions focus on young contemporary artists. The same building also contains the Kunsthalle.

66_67 ▽

Grabbeplatz · Der Grabbeplatz vereint Architektur aus etwa 350 Jahren: die Andreaskirche aus dem 17. Jahrhundert, das ehemalige wilhelminische Amts- und Landgericht, die Kunsthalle aus den 60er-Jahren und den postmodernen Baustil des K20. Ferner sieht man darüber hinaus als eines der bedeutendsten Gebäude der Nachkriegsmoderne und als Symbol des Wirtschaftswunders das Dreischeibenhaus. Die städtische Oper und der Hofgarten vervollständigen einige der wichtigsten kulturellen und naturnahen Freizeitmöglichkeiten der Stadt.

Grabbeplatz · This square combines architectural highlights from a period of time over 350 years – St. Andreas church from the 17th century, the former local and regional court dating back to Wilhelminian times, Kunsthalle built in the 1960s and K20-museum representing post-modern style. If you lift your gaze and look up in the sky, you will see another construction that made architectural history – the Dreischeibenhaus. The office building was considered to symbolise the economic miracle of post-war Germany.

K20 · In ihrem Wunsch, der Stadt ein stärkeres kulturpolitisches Profil zu verleihen, gründete die nordrhein-westfälische Landesregierung 1961 die Kunstsammlung NRW als privatrechtliche Stiftung. Diese besteht mittlerweile aus drei Häusern: dem K20, dem K21 in Hafennähe und dem Schmela-Haus in der Altstadt. Mit der Eröffnung des K20 im schwarzen Granitbau 1986 in unmittelbarer Nähe zur Kunstakademie knüpfte die Stadt damit an Düsseldorfs Rolle in der Kunstförderung seit der ersten Gemäldegalerie unter Jan Wellem an. Die umfassende ständige Sammlung des K20 bietet einen einzigartigen Blick in die Klassische Moderne. Paul Klee und Piet Mondrian sind genauso vertreten wie Robert Rauschenberg und Andy Warhol als Ikonen der Pop-Art. Sehenswerte Ausstellungen der vergangenen Jahre befassten sich u.a. mit Joseph Beuys und Katharina Fritsch.

K20 · Aspiring to raise the cultural profile of the city government, the state of North Rhine-Westphalia founded the Kunstsammlung NRW as an art foundation run under private law in 1961. It has since developed into an collection of three museums – K20, K21 near the Media Harbour and Schmela Haus in the Old Town. When, in 1986, the city celebrated the K20's opening in the black granite building close to the city's arts academy, it was only continuing the city's supportive role since Prince Elector Jan Wellem initiated the first art gallery. The K20's permanent collection offers an extensive insight into modern art. Pay it a visit to find paintings by Paul Klee, Piet Mondrian, Robert Rauschenberg and Andy Warhol, to name just a few. Recent exhibitions displayed works of art by Joseph Beuys and Katharina Fritsch.

Kom(m)ödchen · Die Erfolgsgeschichte des 1949 gegründeten, politisch-literarischen Kabaretts ist ungebrochen, Veranstaltungen sind oft über Monate im Voraus ausgebucht. Kay und Lore Lorentz führten es bis in die 60er-Jahre hinein gemeinsam, bevor Lore eine Solo-Karriere startete. Nach dem Tod ihres Mannes 1993 führte sie für kurze Zeit wieder die Umsetzung der geplanten Stücke weiter, bevor ihr Sohn nach ihrem Tod die Leitung übernahm. Die oft anspielungsreichen Inhalte der Darbietungen sorgten sowohl bei der Regierung, der damalige Verteidigungsminister Franz-Josef Strauß untersagte 1959 die Fernsehübertragungen, als auch bei der das Programm als zu »systemstabilisierend« bezeichnenden Studentenschaft der 60er-Jahre für Kritik. Das Theater befindet sich seit 1967 auf der Rückseite des Quaderbaus der Kunsthalle und des Kunstvereins.

Kom(m)ödchen · The success story of one of Germany's most famous political and literary cabarets is unbroken. Since its opening in 1949 it has gained an almost legendary reputation and performances are often sold out months ahead. Founders Kay and Lore Lorentz first ran this theatre together, before Lore began her solo career in the 1960s. For a short while, she resumed her office as director when her husband died in 1993, passing the business on to her son upon her own death. The content of the performances has often been controversial and generated criticism both among the government and the students in the 1960s. The theatre is located in the heart of the Old Town in the same grey cube building as the Kunsthalle and the Kunstverein.

Ehrenhof · Zur Düsseldorfer Museenlandschaft gehört genau zwischen Hofgarten und Rheinufer liegend ein Areal, das bei seinem ersten Zweck ein Publikumsmagnet sondergleichen war: 1926 fand hier die größte Messe der Weimarer Republik, die sogenannte »GeSoLei« (Große Ausstellung für Gesundheitspflege, soziale Fürsorge und Leibesübungen) statt, die 7,5 Mio. Besucher anzog und sich ursprünglich über eine 2 km lange Strecke parallel zum Rhein erstreckte. Der Name Ehrenhof erinnert an den von Gebäudeflügeln dreiseitig umschlossenen Empfangshof symmetrischer Schlossanlagen. In dem expressionistischen Gebäudekomplex sind mit dem Museum Kunstpalast und dem NRW-Forum Institutionen verschiedener Kunstrichtungen untergebracht. Auch im Innenhof zwischen und an den Gebäuden befinden sich Kunstwerke mit Erzählcharakter.

Ehrenhof · If you look at the rather quiet museum area located right between Hofgarten and Rhine river today, you might not believe that upon its opening in 1926, it attracted 7.5 million visitors. The reason for this unexpected ‚invasion' was that its initial purpose was to host the largest exhibition for health, social welfare and physical activity during the Weimar Republic. The total fairground stretched over a distance of 2 kilometres along the Rhine river. The word Ehrenhof normally signifies the three-winged reception-enclosure of a symmetrical castle ground. In Düsseldorf, this expressionist style establishment nowadays comprises several museums with collections ranging from the Middle Ages to contemporary arts. The courtyard between the buildings also contains a variety of sculptures that all have a story to tell.

Museum Kunstpalast · Seit 2001 wird der Museumskomplex am Ehrenhof als sogenannte »Public-private-partnership« gemeinsam von einer Stiftung der Stadt, dem
Energieunternehmen EON sowie dem Handelskonzern Metro Group getragen. Er
vereint in den ehemaligen Bauten der Ausstellung »GeSoLei« verschiedene Kunstrichtungen: Die Hauptsammlung besteht aus Werken vom Mittelalter bis zur Gegenwart,
während Spezialsammlungen von Kunsthandwerk über Grafikdesign bis hin zu bedeu-
tender Glaskunst reichen. Der Grundstock der ständigen Sammlung umfasst mit zwei
Rubensgemälden auch die Zeit des Kurfürsten Jan Wellem, der als großer Förderer der
Kunst gemeinsam mit seiner Frau Anna Maria Luisa de Medici die erste Gemäldegalerie der Stadt eröffnete. Weitere wesentliche Bestandteile sind Werke der Düsseldorfer
Malerschule und des Jungen Rheinlands.

Museum Kunstpalast · Since 2001 this comprehensive museum has been run as a
public private partnership supported by a community foundation and two large
corporations which have their headquarters in Düsseldorf – EON and Metro Group.
The expressionist buildings that initially used to be parts of a fair ground for the
greatest exhibition of the nation in 1926 nowadays contain several art collections.
While the heart of the collection comprises pieces of art ranging from the Middle
Ages to the present, certain rooms are assigned to handicraft, graphic design and
glass. Two paintings by Flemish artist Peter Paul Rubens have gained fame due to
the fact that Prince Elector Jan Wellem acquired them for the city's first art gallery.
Do not miss important pieces of art from Düsseldorfer Malerschule and
Junges Rheinland.

Tonhalle · Wo früher Sterne zu sehen waren, treten heute Stars auf. Vom Innenhof des Ehrenhofs ausgehend liegt die Tonhalle genau am südlichen Ende der Sichtachse. 1926 im Rahmen des für die »GeSoLei« errichteten Gebäudekomplexes Ehrenhof, findet man heute immer noch Elemente, die auf ihre erste Nutzung als Planetarium hindeuten: der vergoldete Stern an der Kuppelspitze sowie Skulpturen-Paare an der Freitreppe zum Ehrenhof hin. Das einstige Foyer (»Grünes Gewölbe«) der ehemaligen »Rheinhalle« mit der türkisen Kuppel beherbergt einige Glaskunstwerke aus der Sammlung Hentrich, die mit zum Museum Kunstpalast gehört. Erst 1976 wurde der Bau von Wilhelm Kreis, bekannt für seine Monumentalarchitektur, nach der teilweisen Zerstörung im Zweiten Weltkrieg wieder instand gesetzt. Heute sitzt man bei den meist klassischen Konzerten wieder unter einem Sternenhimmel.

Tonhalle · This building located at the South End of Ehrenhof near the Rhine river has always been featuring stars. Initially built as part of the great fair for health, social welfare and physical activity in 1926, it first served as a planetarium – a fact commemorated by a golden star on top of its dome as well as some sculptures along the outside steps symbolising several planets. Nowadays visitors to Tonhalle are delighted by live stars performing classical concerts by reputable solo artists and internationally well-known orchestras. The guests will also get to see some selected pieces of glass art which are part of a permanent glass collection in Museum Kunstpalast only a couple of hundred meters away. The Tonhalle was partly damaged in WWII and rebuilt only in 1976.

Tonhalle · 1854 Zuschauer finden im großen Saal der Tonhalle am Ehrenhof Platz. 2005 nutzte man eine notwendig gewordene Brandschutz- und Asbestsanierung zur kompletten Neugestaltung. Seit den 70er-Jahren hat sich die Anzahl der Konzerte auf mittlerweile etwa 300 Termine mit über 300.000 Besuchern pro Jahr gesteigert. Die Installation von Schallumlenkkörpern in der Innenkuppel bietet eine ideale Akustik, nicht nur für klassische Konzerte. Die Düsseldorfer Symphoniker teilen ihr »Zuhause« u.a. mit dem London Symphony Orchestra und dem Klavierstar Lang Lang. Besonderes »Highlight« sind die Lichtkunstwerke unter der Kuppel, die an die ursprüngliche Funktion der Tonhalle erinnern.

Tonhalle · The big concert hall located near the museum area at Ehrenhof by the Rhine river offers room for up to 1854 fans of mostly classical music. After serving as a multi-purpose hall at the big exhibition it had been built for, it used to be a planetarium for a couple of years. Since the reconstruction of the war-damaged building in 1976, the number of mostly classical music events has now reached about 300 per year, delighting more than 300,000 listeners. Special sound elements contribute to an excellent acoustics. Düsseldorf's Symphonic Orchestra share their home with such celebrities as The London Symphonic Orchestra and Chinese star pianist Lang Lang. A recent renovation of the concert hall included the installation of "star lights" under the rooftop and thus guarantees its guests a "heavenly" experience.

Oper · Die Deutsche Oper am Rhein blickt auf eine langjährige Kooperation der Städte Düsseldorf und Duisburg zurück. Das Opernhaus an der Heinrich-Heine-Allee erhielt sein heutiges Gesicht Mitte der 50er-Jahre, nachdem es im Zweiten Weltkrieg weitgehend zerstört worden war. 1875 wurde an diesem Standort das neue Stadttheater im Stil der Neurenaissance eröffnet, das seinen Bauplatz auf einem Stück des Botanischen Gartens fand. Das Vorderhaus des Baus steht heute unter Denkmalschutz.

Opera · The Deutsche Oper am Rhein serves as an excellent example of a successful cooperation between cultural institutions of two cities – Düsseldorf and Duisburg. Theatre and opera have always been related in Düsseldorf – the property at Heinrich-Heine Allee bordering Hofgarten where today's opera house is located used to be the ground of the renaissance-style theatre building which opened in 1875. After being severely damaged during WWII, it was rebuilt in the 1950s. Its front part is now classified as a protected historical monument.

82_83 ▽

Oper · In der Saison 2006/2007 feierte die Deutsche Oper am Rhein ihr 50. Bühnenjubiläum. Die erste Spielzeit 1956 wurde in Düsseldorf mit der Oper »Elektra« eingeläutet. Seitdem erfreut das Haus seine Gäste mit einem vielfältigen, anspruchsvollen Programm. Neben klassischen Opernaufführungen, hält das Haus mit einer Ballettgruppe die Zuschauer in Atem: 45 Tänzerinnen und Tänzer aus 16 Nationen machen das Ensemble aus, das sich mit Auftritten weltweit einen Namen gemacht hat.

Opera · Düsseldorf celebrated the 50th stage anniversary of the Deutsche Oper am Rhein in 2006/2007. The performance of »Elektra« was the kick-off event in Düsseldorf in 1956. The institution has been delighting its audience with a versatile and sophisticated program. It not only offers classical operas, but both Düsseldorf and Duisburg take great pride in their ballet cast – 45 dancers from 16 countries have gained worldwide fame.

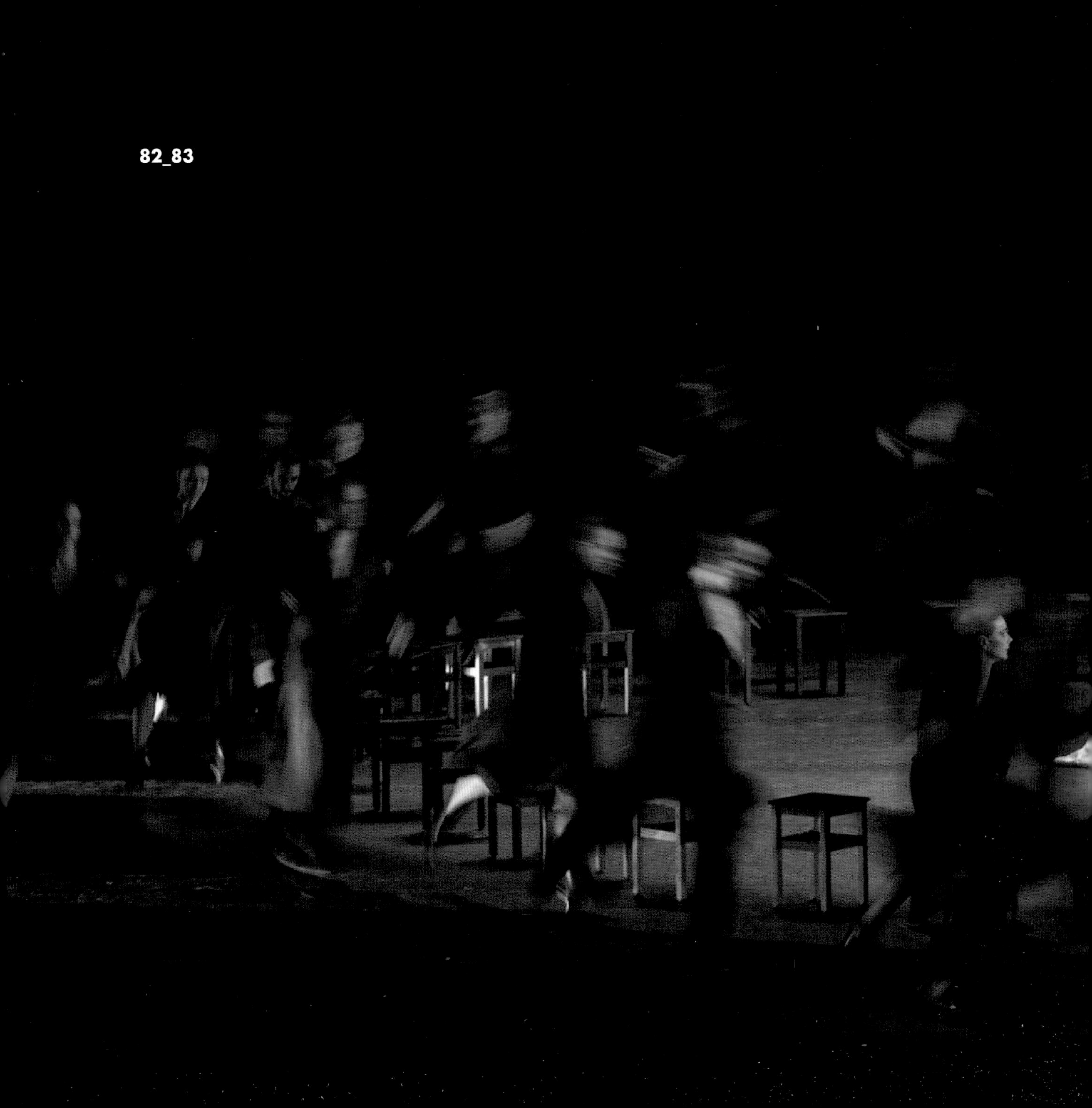

Kunstakademie · »Für unsere Studenten nur das Beste« – so lautet der in die Eingangs-
treppe eingemeißelte Anspruch der 1773 gegründeten Akademie. Der aus der Neo-
renaissance stammende Bau befindet sich ummittelbar zwischen Rhein und Altstadt und
bringt seit Jahrhunderten als Lern- und Lehrstätte bedeutende Künstler hervor. Paul Klee
und August Macke waren hier genauso tätig wie Gerhard Richter und Günter Uecker.
Dabei war die Akademie Keimzelle verschiedener Kunstrichtungen wie z.B. der
Düsseldorfer Malerschule, ZERO und Fluxus, die ihr internationale Berühmtheit ver-
liehen. Immer wieder ist sie für spektakuläre Aktionen und Diskurse gut, die für Schlag-
zeilen sorgen, nicht zuletzt durch den auch für seine Fettecke berühmten Künstler
Joseph Beuys, dem hier zeitweilig die Professur aberkannt wurde.

Kunstakademie · Stakes are high at Düsseldorf's art academy – "Only the best for
our students" is what every visitor reads when taking the stairs to the entrance of this
famous educational institute found in 1773. The neo-renaissance-style school is located
between the Old Town and the Rhine and was the breeding ground for many famous
artists such as Paul Klee, August Macke, Gerhard Richter and Günther Uecker, to name
just a few. Several well-known styles found their origins in this building – Düsseldorfer
Malerschule, ZERO and Fluxus have gained international recognition. From time to
time, the academy gets media attention not only for the obvious, but made the head-
lines for example when artist and professor Joseph Beuys was temporarily dismissed
for taking political action to support his students.

Johanneskirche · Die größte evangelische Stadtkirche St. Johannes liegt in unmittelbarer Nähe zur Königsallee am Martin-Luther-Platz. Hier erinnert Düsseldorf mit drei
Statuen von Reichskanzler von Bismarck, Kaiser Wilhelm und General von Moltke
an drei große Staatsmänner. Seit 1994 gilt die Aufmerksamkeit der Passanten jedoch
eher den angrenzenden Schadow-Arkaden, wo sie sich shopping-technisch und
kulinarisch verausgaben können.

Johanneskirche · St. Johannes church is the largest protestant church in the city centre
and is located at Martin-Luther-Platz in direct vicinity to Königsallee. The square also
features statues of three big statesmen – chancellor Otto von Bismarck, William the
Emperor and General von Moltke. However, most passers-by lay greater focus on the
nearby Schadow-Arkaden – a shopping mall built in 1994, offering attractive shopping and dining opportunities

88_89 ▽

Schauspielhaus/Dreischeibenhaus · Am Gustaf-Gründgens-Platz stehen zwei
Bauten in spannungsreichem Kontrast zueinander: Links das Dreischeibenhaus,
lange Zeit nach seinem früheren Nutzer auch Thyssen-Haus genannt, rechts das
Düsseldorfer Schauspielhaus. Die skulpturale Großform des Theaterbaus entstand
1965-69. Heute erfreut das Ensemble im »Großen« und im »Kleinen Haus« sein
Publikum mit klassischen und modernen Stücken.

Schauspielhaus/Dreischeibenhaus · If you want to observe the tension created by
two different architectural styles, walk to Gustaf-Gründgens Platz near Hofgarten
and position yourself between two buildings which have gone down in history.
The left one measures 94 m, seems to consist of three sheets of different heights
(Dreischeibenhaus). The low, curved theatre building to your right caused a lot of
arguments when it overrun the initially planned construction costs in the 1960s.
The Düsseldorfer Schauspielhaus is pleases its audience with a wide range of plays.

88_89

Königsallee · Das Einkaufsparadies für Gutbetuchte ist in den vergangenen Jahren nicht billiger und nicht leerer geworden! Luxusketten wie Gucci, Versace, Dior und Hermès scheuen nicht vor den horrenden Ladenmieten zurück, während einige alt-eingesessene Familienunternehmen kürzlich die Pforten schließen mussten. »Sehen und gesehen werden« ist hier das Motto. Neuestes Ziel zur »gepflegten Verausga-bung« ist der »Kö-Bogen« am nördlichen Ende des Prachtboulevards. In den beiden Gebäudeteilen befindet sich neben dem Luxuskaufhaus Breuninger und diversen Geschäften für die edle Ausstattung auch gehobene italienische Gastronomie.

Königsallee · If you want to do some extensive shopping, spend a lot of money and watch some posh ladies walk past, Königsallee is the place to go. Recently, some top fashion chains such as Hermès and Dior have opened new stores while some traditional family businesses had to close their doors. See and be seen is still a motto people have been following to a great extent. Those with a substantial amount of money to spend have recently found a new destination to exchange it for something precious – the Kö-Bogen, a new archtitectural highlight was opened in 2013.

Kö-Graben · Der einen Kilometer lange Prachtboulevard zieht Menschen aus aller Welt zum Einkaufsbummel an. Auf Geheiß der Franzosen nach dem »Frieden von Lunéville« wurde die Befestigungsanlage der Stadt geschliffen und nach Plänen eines Verschönerungskomitees durch einen Stadtgraben ersetzt, damals noch als Allee an der östlichen Stadtgrenze.

Kö-Graben · One of Germany's top shopping boulevards is not merely a street lined with shops. This charming avenue is lined with huge old trees, gravel walkways and picturesque sculptures and even has a well-kept canal running down its middle. Invisible now, this boulevard was built on the former fortification of the city.

Einkaufszentren · Schadow-Arkaden, Kö-Galerie, Sevens und Stilwerk – sowohl architektonisch als auch vom Verkaufsangebot her unterscheiden sich die stylischen Einkaufszentren direkt an oder ganz in der Nähe der Königsallee von so manchen anderen anonymen Shoppingmalls in der Umgebung. Mit ihren gläsernen Kuppeln und den oft runden Formen erinnern sie eher an Galerien. Auch das Angebot an Modegeschäften und Gastronomie ist zwischen mittlerem und gehobenem Niveau anzusiedeln. Das »Stilwerk« in der Grünstraße, wo sich bis in die 80er-Jahre ein Wellenbad befand, bietet Einrichtungsgeschäfte der Luxusbranche. Die 1994 eröffneten Schadow-Arkaden finden sogar noch Platz für ein Fitnessstudio und ein Boulevard-Theater sowie das Pressehaus der Rheinischen Post.

Shopping Malls · Forget about the anonymity of typical shopping malls. Düsseldorf features four combinations of both architectural and shopping highlights all in direct vicinity to each other. Directly on or near Königsallee, they were all developed and partly reconstructed within the last 30 years. Glass domes, arcades, lots of transparency and atriums contribute to turning your shopping into a sightseeing experience as well. Each one of them has a different focus, but they all include middle-class to high-end brands and food courts. Schadow-Arkaden might feature the most affordable fashion chains among the four, while Kö-Galerie and Sevens include premium-priced designer brands and jewellers. The four floors in Stilwerk on Grünstraße are occupied by furniture stores. Its lobby displays the most glamorous Christmas tree from November on.

Libeskind-Bauten · Die großräumige Veränderung der prominenten Stelle am Ende der Königsallee wurde von Seiten nicht weniger Bürger zunächst von Protesten begleitet. Im Gegensatz zu früher hat man seit der Fertigstellung des ersten Teils 2013 jetzt zwar vom Schadow-Platz aus keinen freien Blick mehr auf den Hofgarten. Das »Tor zum Hofgarten« bringt das Credo des bekannten New Yorker Architekten Daniel Libeskind zum Ausdruck, nach dem eine Stadt vor allem den Menschen dienen solle.

Libeskind Buildings · When you are standing in front of the "world's best urban building", you would never believe that up until a couple of years ago, this used to be a major bus and tram station. It was not easy to convince Düsseldorf's citizens to give up on this unimpressive, but useful square offering a view on the city centre's Hofgarten Park. In this construction, the famous architect Daniel Libeskind managed to incorporate his belief that a city should primarily serve its citizens. It is also known as Kö-Bogen and is now located at the northern end of the boulevard.

98_99 ▽

Kö-Bogen · »Raum zum Arbeiten und Entspannen« – so warb die Stadt mit den Plänen für die Neugestaltung des Areals zwischen Hofgarten und Schadow-Arkaden. Die entstandene Kombination aus Ladenlokalen, Büroflächen und Gastronomie inmitten von großzügigen Freiflächen zum Spazieren und Ausruhen scheint dies auf ideale Weise zu erfüllen. Namhafte Mieter bewohnen die beiden Gebäudehälften. Die Freitreppe am Wasserbecken bietet die beste Aussicht sowohl auf den Hofgarten als auch auf die schmucke Stein- und Glasfassade.

Kö-Bogen · "Space to work and relax" was the slogan the city used to promote their plans to completely reconstruct the area between Hofgarten Park and Schadow Arkaden shopping mall. It seems that the result, consisting of a combination of shops, office space, and large areas to stroll around and relax, appears to fulfil just that. The tenants which have turned "Königsallee 2" into their prominent business address are mostly just as well-known. During good weather, the spacious steps above the water basin facing Hofgarten serve many people as benches to relax.

Steigenberger Parkhotel · Die heutige Postadresse des zunächst unter »Grand Hotel« am Corneliusplatz 1 firmierenden Hauses, »Königsallee 1a«, unterstreicht den exklusiven Charakter der 5-Sterne-Einrichtung. Das Steigenberger wirbt nicht nur mit seinem schönen Blick auf den Hofgarten, sondern auch durch die unmittelbare Nähe zum kulturellen und geschäftlichen Zentrum der Stadt. 1902 wurde das Hotel für die in Düsseldorf stattfindende Industrie- und Gewerbe-Ausstellung errichtet und hat seitdem viele prominente Gäste gesehen, darunter auch Thomas Mann, der seine Eindrücke in einem Roman verarbeitete. Ebenfalls in dem Gebäude befindet sich der Industrie-Club Düsseldorf, wo Adolf Hitler 1932 eine einflussreiche Rede gehalten hat. 119 Zimmer, 11 Suiten, 9 Tagungsräume und ein moderner Spa-Bereich laden zum mondänen Aufenthalt ein.

Steigenberger Parkhotel · This 5-star hotel knows how to promote their business – what started out as Grand Hotel at Corneliusplatz 1 has now for many years been called Steigenberger Parkhotel and is now registered under "Königsallee 1a" (Königsallee 1 was already being used by their direct neighbour, the Kaufhof department store!). In their advertisements, the hotel focuses on advertising both the pleasant view on Hofgarten-park and the direct vicinity to luxury shopping, business opportunities and cultural institutions. Since its construction in 1902, many famous guests have enjoyed staying at the Steigenberger. The building is also home to Düsseldorf's Industrial Club. It gained fame when Adolf Hitler came to hold a very influential speech there in 1932. 119 rooms, 11 suites and 9 conference rooms are ready to turn your stay in Düsseldorf into an unforgettable event.

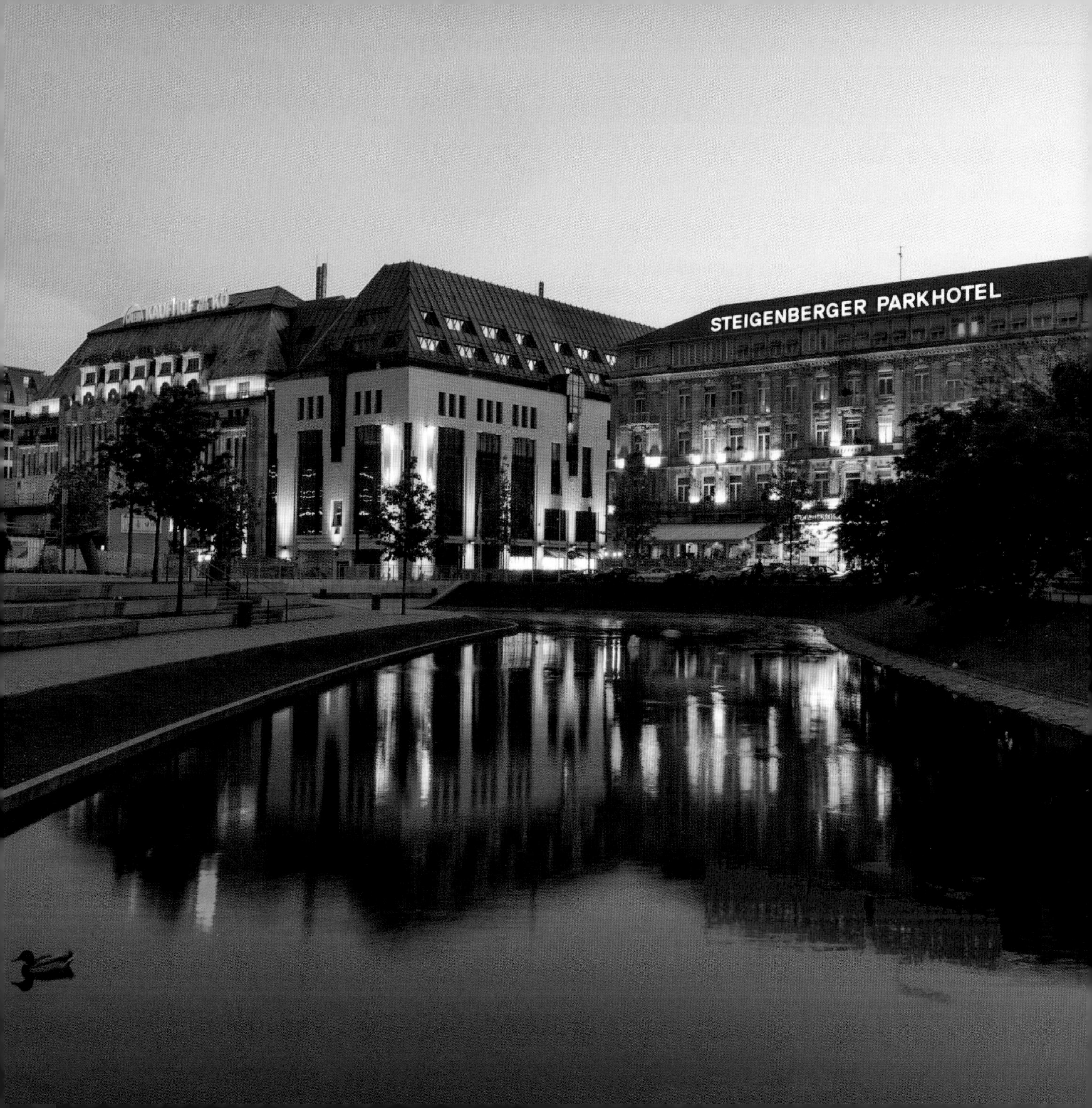
STEIGENBERGER PARKHOTEL

Luxushotels · Drei der Düsseldorfer 5-Sterne-Hotels liegen, praktisch für ihr gut betuchtes Klientel, alle unmittelbar an der Königsallee. Hotels haben vor allem zu Messezeiten in der Stadt Hochkonjunktur und sind trotz der bis auf das Dreifache steigenden Preise oft ausgebucht. Die Konzepte der drei renommierten Häuser sind unterschiedlich ausgerichtet. Der Breidenbacher Hof von 1812 setzt auch nach dem kompletten Neubau 2009 auf individuellen Service und ein goldbraunes Ambiente, das den oft aus arabischen Ländern und Russland stammenden Gästen schmeicheln soll. Während das Steigenberger Parkhotel von 1902 mit einem idyllischen Blick auf den Hofgarten wirbt, geht es beim Inteconti auf der Kö um stylischen Schick, der durch die dazugehörige »Bar Fifty Nine«, bekannt für ihre über 130 Cocktails, unterstützt wird.

Luxury hotels · The market for hotels in Düsseldorf seems to be never-ending – meaning both the number of new hotels and their prices have constantly been rising – especially during times of trade fairs. Three five-star hotels lie at or near Königsallee and are attractive for business people as well as for those wanting to shop or who are visiting Düsseldorf for medical treatment. Their interior designs and service concepts each have a different focus. The golden and brown furnishing style and the individual service of Breidenbacher Hof is especially popular among guests from Russia and the Arab countries. While Steigenberger Parkhotel stresses the great view on Hofgarten-park, Interconti on Königsallee attracts people who appreciate modern-style architecture and an opportunity to chill out at trendy Bar Fifty Nine, famous for offering 130 different cocktails.

Hofgarten · Deutschlands ältester Volksgarten befindet sich in Düsseldorf. Die »grüne Lunge«, die sich vom Rhein aus an der Altstadt entlang erstreckt, ist eine rund 27 Hektar große Fläche, die mit ihren Wiesen, Bäumen, Spielplätzen, Spazierwegen und Bänken Erholung für alle bietet. Ende des 18. Jahrhunderts regte Graf von Goltstein bei der kurfürstlichen Regierung zahlreiche Maßnahmen zur Verbesserung der durch Krieg und Missernten maroden Stadt an. Durch den Umbau des ehemals fürstlichen Hofgartens zur öffentlichen Promenade schuf man nicht nur Arbeitsplätze, sondern verband auch das damals noch außerhalb liegende Schloss Jägerhof mit der Stadt. Skulpturen wie der »Märchenbrunnen« und der »Gröne Jong« beleben den Park, der einen barocken Gartenstil im älteren Teil mit dem eines englischen Landschaftsgartens im neueren Teil kombiniert.

Hofgarten · Calling it "the Central Park of Düsseldorf" would be a bit exaggerated, but Düsseldorf's green spot lies directly next to the business and shopping district and both the Old Town and Rhine are close to its borders. It comprises an area of 27 hectares and with its many lawns, trees, playgrounds, walkways and benches everyone will find their favourite spot. Its existence is due to the initiative of a local Duke who requested to his superiors that Düsseldorf's appearance be improved after the city had suffered significantly from war and crop failure in the 18th century. Its first purpose of a princely park was then turned into the nation's first recreational area for the common people. At the same time, the reconstruction meant creating many jobs. Several picturesque sculptures contribute to making a stroll through the park into an interesting experience.

Ständehaus · Das wunderschöne, 1876-80 im Stil der italienischen Hochrenaissance als Parlamentsgebäude des preußischen Provinziallandtags erbaute jetzige Museum »K21« lässt vermuten, dass dort Kunstwerke aus alter Zeit zu bewundern sind. Betritt man das Gebäude, wird schnell deutlich, dass man es hier mit modernster Kunst der Gegenwart zu tun hat. Im Gegensatz zum ebenfalls zur Kunstsammlung NRW gehörenden »K20«, das sich auf Kunst aus dem 20. Jahrhundert konzentriert, findet man hier unter gläserner Kuppel Dauer- und Sonderausstellungen mit zeitgenössischen Werken. Von 1949-88 beherbergte das Gebäude den nordrhein-westfälischen Landtag, bis er seinen Sitz an den Rhein verlegte. Am jeweils ersten Mittwoch im Monat sponsort die Wirtschaftsprüfungsgesellschaft KPMG zwischen 18 und 22 Uhr den freien Eintritt ins K20 und ins K21.

Ständehaus · If you look at the beautiful historicism-style building from a distance, you would expect to find anything but those truly modern pieces of art that are displayed inside. Built between 1876-80, the fascinating construction served as the state parliament from 1949-1988 before the government moved to its new home near the harbour area. In 2002 it was turned into the K21 Museum and became part of the Kunstsammlung NRW, focusing on contemporary artists. While the basement displays changing exhibitions, the upper floors are occupied by the permanent collection. Large sculptures or installations right under the glass dome usually make up the highlight of the institution. The lobby is regularly a venue for prominent business parties. Audit and assurance company KPMG sponsors free admission and special events to visitors every first Wednesday night in the month.

Flughafen Düsseldorf · Der drittgrößte deutsche Flughafen legt seit seiner Namensän-
derung in »Düsseldorf Airport« und mit Festlegung des Logos auf »DUS« noch mehr
Fokus auf seinen Status als internationales Drehkreuz. Jedes Jahr erweitern die rund
80 dort agierenden Fluggesellschaften ihr Liniennetz, sodass 2014 von Düsseldorf
aus 188 Ziele angeflogen werden konnten. Seit seiner Eröffnung 1927 ist die Zahl
der Fluggäste auf fast 22 Mio. pro Jahr gestiegen. Die weitaus meisten Kunden hatte
2014 mit über 7 Mio. airberlin zu verzeichnen. Noch aus zwei anderen Gründen ist
der Flughafen ein wichtiger Wirtschaftsfaktor: Das 365 Tage geöffnete Einkaufszen-
trum »Airport Arkaden« und der anliegende Büro- und Dienstleistungspark
»Düsseldorf Airport City« ziehen über den Flugverkehr hinaus Kunden an.

Düsseldorf Airport · Germany's third largest airport was recently renamed
Düsseldorf Airport with the logo DUS in order to accent its international status.
Around 80 airlines have constantly been expanding their routes. This resulted in
a total of 188 destinations in 2014. Since the airport first opened in 1927, the
amount of traveling guests has risen to almost 22 million per year. Air Berlin,
which call DUS its home airport, accounted for the largest number of guests in 2014
(more than 7 million). Not only for its good international connection has DUS
become an important economic factor: The Airport Arkaden comprise a number of
fashion and accessory shops open to the public 365 days per year. In addition,
the nearby Düsseldorf Airport City is a brand new office and service area which
attracts customers. A sky train quickly transports passengers from nearby train station
to their terminal.

Messe Düsseldorf · Jedes Jahr im Januar gibt es umfangreichen Besuch im Düsseldorfer Norden: Vom Kanu bis zur großen Segelyacht ist alles an Wasserfahrzeugen dabei, was sich die Besucher der weltweit größten Bootsmesse wünschen können. In 17 Messehallen sorgen etwa 1600 Aussteller der »boot« für ein attraktives Programm rund um den Wassersport. Dabei ist die Ausrüstung für den Segelsport genauso im Angebot wie Wasserski und die neueste Angeltechnik. Zum Testen wird ausdrücklich eingeladen – etwa im Tauchturm oder auf der Kanustrecke. Sowohl was den Umsatz als auch was die Fläche betrifft, rangiert Düsseldorf weltweit als fünftgrößte Messe. Mehr als 40 Messen finden jährlich hier statt, von denen 22 Weltleitcharakter haben. Dazu gehören die Druckmesse drupa, die Verpackungsmesse Interpack und die Kunststoffmesse K.

Düsseldorf Trade Fair · If you are interested in any kind of hobby related to ships or water, the boot trade fair is the place to go every year around the end of January. Whether it is a canoe or a giant yacht you are looking for – boot has it all in one of the 17 halls that make up the Düsseldorf Trade Fair ground north of the city centre. 1600 exhibitors display their businesses and contribute to an attractive fair program reaching from diving attempts in a special tower or testing a canoe on an appropriate course. As far as turnover and size are concerned, Düsseldorf is currently ranking fifth on a worldwide scale. It hosts around 40 trade fairs every year, some of them on an annual basis. Others take place every three years. 22 are considered to be the leading ones in their industry. Big names are drupa (print), Interpack (packaging) and K (plastics).

GAP · Fast schon nach Verhüllungskunst à la Christo sah es aus: Zweimal in seiner Geschichte hatten die Düsseldorfer die Gelegenheit, das 90 m hohe Bürogebäude an der prominenten Adresse Graf-Adolf-Platz 15 (GAP) verschleiert zu bewundern. Noch während der Bauarbeiten 2005 und noch einmal genau sechseinhalb Jahre später fielen bei einem Sturm Fensterelemente in gegenüberliegende Gebäude, sodass man es danach monatelang nur grün verschleiert bewundern konnte.
Der moderne, 24-geschossige Teil dieser Gebäudekombination scheint gegenüber dem fünfstöckigen Flachbau, der die denkmalgeschützte Fassade des ehemaligen Fernmeldeamtes enthält, der wesentlich anfälligere dieser Symbiose aus Alt und Neu zu sein. Das architektonische Highlight am südlichen Ende der Kö beherbergt u.a. die Unternehmensberatung Ernst & Young sowie gehobene Gastronomie.

GAP · The green veil that seemed to be hiding one of the city's new office buildings and architectural highlights was not there for decoration purposes, but for protection instead. Twice since 2005, several windows fell from the glass facade of GAP 15 (named after the postal address Graf-Adolf-Platz 15). The building combination consists of two parts – one being a 24-storey modern eclipse-shaped tower, and the other one being a five-storey, flat, classical-style building that is protected as a historical monument. The latter one used to be the city's telecommunications office. This symbiosis of old and new architecture is located at the southern end of Königs-allee and home to companies such as Ernst & Young and some restaurants.

Esprit-Arena · Die Multifunktionsarena im Stadtteil Stockum hat schon viel gesehen: Große Sportveranstaltungen finden hier genauso statt wie Popkonzerte internationaler Musikgrößen. Bekanntester Nutzer ist der durch Höhen und Tiefen gegangene lokale Fußballverein Fortuna Düsseldorf, der hier seine Gäste zu Heimspielen empfängt und sich einer großen Fangemeinde erfreut. Die findet Platz auf maximal 54.600 Plätzen, was die Arena zum achtgrößten Fußballstadion Deutschlands macht. Es entstand 2002-2004 und ersetzte das vorherige Rheinstadion. In seiner Umgebung befinden sich nicht nur Flughafen und Messegelände, sondern auch ein großes Schwimmbad, eine Tartanbahn, ein 3-Sterne-Hotel und Rasenplätze. International in den Medien war die damals umbenannte »Düsseldorf Arena« nicht zuletzt 2011, als der Eurovision Song Contest hier ausgetragen wurde.

Esprit-Arena · Since a major makeover of the former Rheinstadion in 2004, Düsseldorf has been proud owner of a multifunctional sports arena ranking eighth among the nation's soccer stadiums. Fortuna Düsseldorf, the local soccer club, are currently going through a tough time, but are still attracting a large number of local fans to their training and playing grounds. In direct vicinity to Düsseldorf's fairgrounds in the north of the city centre, the arena offers space for 54600 spectators and features a retractable roof. From the stadium, visitors will not only reach Düsseldorf Airport within minutes, but also find an Olympic-sized indoor pool, a tartan track, a three-star hotel and several playing fields. In 2011, the temporarily renamed "Düsseldorf Arena" became famous to the world when staging the Eurovision Song Contest.

Galopprennbahn Grafenberg · Wandert man nordöstlich der Innenstadt im Grafenberger Wald einen der schönen Wege hinauf, stößt man auf die idyllisch gelegene Grafenberger Galopprennbahn. Kurz vor dem Ersten Weltkrieg gebaut, weist das Gelände noch einige aus dieser Zeit stammende, nun unter Denkmalschutz stehende Gebäude auf, allen voran die sogenannte Jockey-Waage. Die moderne Haupttribüne gibt es erst seit 1989, und bei den im Sommer regelmäßig stattfindenden Rennen trifft man hier nicht nur sportliche Prominenz. Rund 8000 Besucher finden durchschnittlich den Weg zu z.T. hochdotierten Veranstaltungen wie dem »Preis der Diana«. Der Innenraum der Rennbahn wird übrigens von einem Golfclub genutzt, der neben der Haupttribüne auch ein Clubhaus mit Restaurant besitzt. Pferde, Reiter und Golfspieler werden hier zur gegenseitigen Rücksichtnahme angehalten.

Galopprennbahn Grafenberg · Düsseldorf has a lot of green natural space to offer, of which the Grafenberg Forest in the north-east of the city centre makes up a large percentage. Located on top is Düsseldorf's horse racing track – an area dating back to the early 20th century and still containing several of the first buildings. They are now under protection as a historical monument, the jockey scale being the most prominent one. The roofed bleachers can host up to 8000 spectators. Between May and October, there are regular horse racing events such as "Preis der Diana" which cause a lot of cars and also some well-dressed ladies and gentlemen to find their way into what is normally a rather quiet area. If you are not into equestrian sports, you might like to take a few shots on the golf course right in the middle of the racing track.

Botanischer Garten · Als Wahrzeichen des 1974 gegründeten Botanischen Gartens der Heinrich-Heine-Universität gilt das gläserne Kuppelgewächshaus. 8 Hektar groß erstreckt sich der Garten auf dem Universitätsgelände am Himmelgeister Landbogen im Süden Düsseldorfs. Neben dem 18 m hohen Glasbau bietet er noch zahlreiche andere Sehenswürdigkeiten, die nicht nur die Studenten zum Forschen anregen – darunter etwa das Rhododendron-Tal, das Südafrika-Haus und der Bauern- und Apothekergarten. Von den rund 70.000 Besuchern im Jahr ist niemand auf sich selbst gestellt: Professionelle Führer zeigen einige der ca. 6000 Pflanzenarten und referieren z.B. über Bibelpflanzen, Gartengestaltung und Pflanzengeographie. Der Schwerpunkt liegt auf den Pflanzen der gemäßigten Klimazonen.

Botanical Garden · Düsseldorf is also a university town and this University (named after famous poet Heinrich Heine) features a green space worth visiting – the Botanical Garden. Founded in 1974, it features lots of precious points of interest – the most famous one being the greenhouse which is 18 m tall and has a dome. The whole garden comprises an area of 8 hectares and is located in the south of the city. The showplaces include a rhodendron valley, a South Africa house, and a farmer's yard. Not only students, but all visitors are encouraged to explore. If you require help or would like to find out more, professional guides are available for taking you on a tour. Apart from telling you in detail about some of the 6,000 different species, they also offer information on "plants from the bible" or geographical conditions.

Japaner in Düsseldorf · Dass in und um Düsseldorf über 8000 Japaner leben, ist im Stadtbild nicht nur im Stadtzentrum an den vielen japanischen Restaurants erkennbar, auch Niederkassel und der Nordpark werden durch landschaftliche und kulturelle Einrichtungen bereichert. Im Nordpark befindet sich seit 1975 ein Geschenk der Japaner: ein 5000 Quadratmeter großer Garten, der die japanische Tradition widerspiegelt, die Natur in idealisierter Weise darzustellen. Landschafts-gärtner reisen extra aus dem Land der untergehenden Sonne an, um u.a. dem Fächerahorn einen speziellen Schnitt zu geben. Auf der anderen Seite des Rheins findet die japanische Bevölkerung in ihrem Wohngebiet ein EKÔ-Haus mit buddhisti-schem Tempel sowie Bibliothek und Kindergarten. Düsseldorf und das Ruhrgebiet gelten als wirtschaftlich guter Standort für japanische Firmen.

Japanese people in Düsseldorf · Once you set foot in the City, it is difficult to miss the Japanese. More than 8,000 of them live in the Düsseldorf area and hold responsible for it featuring the second largest community in Europe. Their residential area is located in Niederkassel, a district on the opposite side of the Rhine river, and i ncludes a school and a temple. A large number of Japanese restaurants and shops can be found close to the city centre. In 1975, the Japanese Ambassador gave a beautiful present to the city to support the friendly business relationship the two nations have been sharing. The Japanese Garden in Nordpark reflects many of the typical styles and traditions of its people. On 5,000 m² visitors are delighted to find special trees that require skilled gardeners' care, as well as little bridges and water fountains.

Nordpark · Den Anlass für den Bau des Nordparks kennt heute kaum noch jemand: 1937 fand in Düsseldorf die Reichsausstellung »Schaffendes Volk« statt, zu der mit fast 7 Mio. Menschen eine riesige Besucherzahl die breit angelegten Wege bevölkerte. Den Hauptteil machten die umstrittenen Skulpturen aus, von denen heute noch einige zu sehen sind, gesäumt von Grün- und Brunnenanlagen, Pavillons und Licht- und Wasserspielen. Besondere Attraktionen sind seit 1975 bzw. 1987 der Japanische Garten mit kleinen Brücken und fein geschnittenen Bäumen sowie das Aquazoo Löbbecke Museum. Mit mehreren Ausgängen Richtung Rhein, Innenstadt und Messegelände ist der Park für jeden gut zugänglich. Sehenswert sind auch der ehemalige »Ballsaal«, heute ein Ausstellungsraum für wechselnde Kunstwerke, und ein prachtvolles Blumenrondell.

Nordpark · Few people know the occasion on which this beautiful park in the North of the city centre was built. In 1937 Düsseldorf was to host a large exhibition for the whole German Reich, displaying the working people. Almost 7 million visitors populated the broad walkways. Sculptures of the different professions were supposed to be the main focus of the event, turned out to be very controversial. Some of them were retrieved after WWII and bear witness to those times. Waterfountains, lights and pavilions are reminiscent of the original park construction. A rose garden, a flower rondel and a ballroom still attract visitors today. The Aquazoo–Löbbecke-Museum and the Japanese Garden are what comes to people's minds first thing these days when mentioning Nordpark. Several playing fields are used for ballgames today.

Kaiserswerth · Als ältester Stadtteil Düsseldorfs schon wesentlich früher besiedelt als die Altstadt im Stadtzentrum, genießt Dörfchen einen gehobenen Status. Zunächst war es noch eine Insel, die jedoch verlandete. Ende des 7. Jahrhunderts bot sie zuerst dem Heiligen Suitbert einen geeigneten Platz für ein Benediktinerkloster und wurde später als Festung berühmt: Kaiser Barbarossa nutzte die heute noch in Ruinen zu besichtigende »Kaiserpfalz« als Unterkunft. Sehenswert sind außerdem die Basilika St. Suitbertus sowie die historische Altstadt.

Kaiserswerth · Even though Düsseldorf is known to be more than 700 years old, there are districts which are much older, one of them being the town of Kaiserswerth. It first became known when St. Suitbert, a Catholic missionary, found it to be an appropriate place to open a convent. Being an island, it later gained fame as a fortress. Emperor Barbarossa built a castle there that he would use as an accommodation. The ruins of this fortress are worth a visit these days. From there it only takes a short walk to reach another landmark – St. Suitbert Basilica. Keep on walking to reach the scenic historical village centre.

126_127 ▽

Schloss Benrath · Wenn man das im 18. Jahrhundert erbaute Barockschloss im Düsseldorfer Süden betrachtet, scheint es unverständlich, dass der Auftraggeber, Kurfürst Carl Theodor, selbst nur während eines Tagesausflugs hier verweilte. Das bedeutsamste architektonische Gesamtkunstwerk Düsseldorfs zieht Besucher mit dem Lustschloss genauso in seinen Bann wie mit dem umliegenden Park samt Weihern. Das Schloss ist nicht nur in Führungen zugänglich, sondern wird auch für Konzertveranstaltungen genutzt. Darüber hinaus bilden das Museum für Europäische Gartenkunst und das Museum für Naturkunde den Ost- bzw. den Westflügel des Hauptgebäudes.

Schloss Benrath · Can you imagine that Prince Elector Carl Theoder, initiator of this beautiful 18th-century Baroque castle, only paid it a one-day visit? Düsseldorf's most important historical piece of architecture was fave the name to the whole district in the south of the city. It is not only the main building that attracts visitors, but also the surrounding museums and park area.

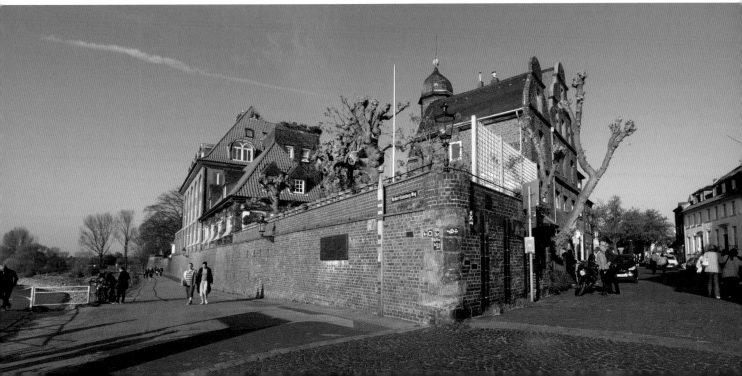